The Football Fan's
Little Instruction Book

The Football Fan's Little Instruction Book

by Giles Greaves

Thorsons
An Imprint of HarperCollins*Publishers*

Thorsons
An Imprint of HarperCollins*Publishers*
77–85 Fulham Palace Road,
Hammersmith, London W6 8JB

Published by Thorsons 1997
1 3 5 7 9 10 8 6 4 2

A catalogue record for this book
is available from the British Library

ISBN 0 7225 3551 1

Printed and bound in Great Britain by
Caledonian International Book Manufacturing Ltd, Glasgow

For Colin, Janet & Hugh
(sorry about the rude bits)

Acknowledgements

Special thanks to Denis Semper and Susan George for hospitality in India while this book was written. Thanks also to Wanda Whiteley and Jo Kyle for asking me to write it and for their peerless support.

Author's Note

Some of my instructions owe their invention to famous personalities in the world of football. Where I know the source, I have given it. Needless to say, 'United', 'City' and 'Rovers' are used for convenience only and do not refer to specific teams!

- Managers: motorway service stations now provide facilities for your dodgy dealings. Just head for the 'coaches only' section.

- Managers are like grapes: put them in the press and you'll always get a good whine.

- Long John Striker: one-footed, a bird on his arm and a blind eye for his team-mates.

No game is complete until the ref has blown up.

Your centre forward is deceptive. He's slower than he looks.

- At 10 to 1, your team seems an excellent value bet for a win. At a quarter to four, it's a different matter.

- Very few players have the courage of their manager's convictions. (Brian Clough)

Dodgy sponsors:

- British Rail – because you've had so many points failures.
- Tampax – because you've had so many bad periods.
- Lucozade – because you're always holding up the table.

- Sketchley – because you're always being taken to the cleaners.
- Bryant & May – because your strikers are always diminutive.
- Senapods – because you've never been tight at the back and you irritate the crap out of the fans.

Be kind to referees: if the weather is hot, give their guide dogs a drink of water.

Footballers may speak in clichés but it's better than letting their goals do the talking.

There are two great teams – the one you support and their reserves.

- Most managers leave because of illness and fatigue: the fans are sick and tired of them.

- It's a pity if you support a Cinderella team: they run away from the ball. But then the coach is a pumpkin.

General elections have been won or lost over the Poor Laws and the Corn Laws, but never the Denis Laws. (Frank Keating)

You can take a donkey to water, but he'd rather have a beer with the rest of the lads.

When you could get drunk on the atmosphere, why does your team have to bottle it?

Some teams are like famous US football stars: they get away with murder at home.

Don't worry if your team's trophy room is burgled – carpets are easily replaceable.

If reincarnation is for real, pray you come back as George Best's fingertips.

Get a new pair of gloves for your dodgy goalkeeper. It's a fair exchange.

Most strikers are like jigsaws: once in the box they go to pieces.

The manager of your team is not the worst in the world. It would be too much of a coincidence.

Footballers are like babies: natural dribblers but likely to s**t themselves when they've got an audience.

⚽ It's a shame when the man you bought to play like a world beater plays like an egg beater. (Barry Fry)

⚽ The '70s-style manager only has a gold Rolls Royce in his garage because he can't wrap it round his finger.

⚽ Bad-boy footballers snort Nutra-Sweet. They think it's diet coke.

⚽ The single soccer fan: 'It's me or the game,' said his partner.

⚽ What do you call a footballer with an IQ of 110? United.

- Some teams are up and down more often than the bog seat in an Indian restaurant.

- There are two types of defender: Abbott and Costello.

- The club chairman: someone let the twat out of the Jag.

- The national team: great on paper, terrible on grass.

- Strikers: remember, your haircut is not just for Christmas.

- Share-holding fans: try to keep the hooligan mentality of the boardroom off the terraces.

A great striker never misses an opening: supermarkets, chip shops, carpet warehouses – he does the lot.

There was a time when you could buy 20 Players for a shilling.

Your new signing: a rat joining a sinking ship.

- Watch out when the team get new metallic strip. They'll try to claim it's 'silverwear'.

- You may not envy your goalkeeper his job, but at least he can touch the bar before the game.

- Half-time entertainment: and you thought things couldn't get any worse.

- Cross a cheetah with a footballer to get a fabulously fast creature which can drink a skinful of lager.

- The new away strip: a load of old Jackson Pollacks.

- Managers: when your chairman says he's right behind you, ask him to stand in front where you can see him. (Tommy Docherty)

- Members of the Mile High Club and Assistant Referees: one's a flight shagger…

- Peter is the patron saint of keepers: when Jesus went for the cross, Peter denied him.

- But keepers, be honest about your abilities: just because Peter was a fisherman, it doesn't mean he'll believe your stories.

Some teams are like bowls of fruit – always on the telly.

If you enjoy reading fiction, always purchase a match day programme.

- Most teams boast a mug in team colours. In fact, some get 40,000 every Saturday.

- Be kind to animals. But request them not to s**t in the away seats.

⚽ Sometimes you will envy a cocktail stick: at least it has two points.

⚽ Sometimes you will envy a lift: at least it doesn't take nine months to go down.

⚽ Sometimes you will envy a two-pin plug: at least it is some use in Europe.

- If cash at the club gets tight, look to the trophy room. There may not be much in it, but antiques fetch good money.

- Spend your holidays by the sea. There are 20,000 leagues and relegation is just a drop in the ocean.

If fans are right about each other, there are either very few virgin sheep or a few very tired ones.

Don't abuse the ref for that penalty decision. Wait for the *Crimewatch* reconstruction.

Tell the team's hard man that he plays like a fairy. Then put the 'phone down.

Things are bad when:

- You dutifully clap for the mascot, until you realise it is the new centre forward.
- Your team signs Steve Davis. They don't just need points, they need snookers.
- Your team trains with traffic cones. The cones win 5–0.

- Your team gets done for tax evasion.
- The announcer asks if there's a goalkeeper in the ground.
- Strangers think your club name ends with 'nil'.
- The manager experiments with 10 at the back.

⚽ 'Is there a doctor in the ground?' Fake an illness to find that fan who will always give you that crucial sick note.

⚽ For that winning goal, edge along a row of seats carrying 12 teas. First-degree burns are a small price to pay.

⚽ The seasonal programme: a whitewash Christmas.

⚽ Buy a set of plastic caricatures of your team. You'll begin to realise how the chairman feels.

⚽ Subbuteo: the only place you'll find a model footballer.

- Relish the noise as you emerge from the tunnel to face the vast Wembley crowd. Then make your way from the tube station to the ground.

- Non-League minnows have a habit of turning into piranhas.

- Pitch invaders went out with Space Invaders.

⚽ If you support a big side, don't be surprised when they run out with bar-codes on their backs.

⚽ You won't find any fair-weather fans to change your light bulb. They all fled at the first sign that it was failing.

Ambassadors for their country abroad do not paint their a**es in team colours and display them to 200 million TV viewers.

Many players are like Laika, the Sputnik dog. They s**t themselves when they find they're in space.

- There are three kinds of footballer: the inspired, the gifted and the majority.

- Help your team out with technical tips, like 'the game has started'. (Ron Atkinson)

- Help your club smash a few records – of the team song.

- Postpone orgasm: try to remember the last time football felt as good as this.

- Footballers are the new rock stars – always caught in possession.

- Behind every great goalkeeper is a better optician.

- Some managers go out like boxers – after taking one cut too many.

- Jock strap: the only supporter a player can really trust.

- Buy a greyhound: that way you might get to Wembley Stadium.

- Hope for a turnaround in your club's fortunes. Where once you were miserable and depressed, you'll now be depressed and miserable.

- If you find a dead Tory MP wearing the rival's strip, dress him in women's underwear to save his family embarrassment.

Dress up as clowns for your last away game. It lifts a team to see fans in replica strip.

Pity the China team: the ball broke off the defender's head and the goalie was chipped.

Every good footballer has an autobiography in him – which is a good place to leave it.

⚽ Playboy footballers: more often scoring on the sheets than on the score sheets.

⚽ There's nothing wrong with a foreign striker that hair clippers can't remedy.

⚽ Many a good football story has been ruined by over attention to the facts.

⚽ Referees: avoid using suppositories. You'll have nowhere to put your cards.

⚽ Footballers' brains are like the prison system – not enough cells per man.

⚽ There is nothing so pleasurable as being miserable with 20,000 others.

- Any fan can afford to be a ball sponsor – but don't expect the player to let you be photographed holding it.

- Veteran footballers: plan for the future. If you get a corner, open a pub on it.

⚽ P**s on your own feet and save a trip to the toilets at half-time.

⚽ If your child wants a cowboy outfit for Christmas, buy him City strip or even the club – whichever is the cheaper.

- Keepers: the wall can't cover the angles when trying to cover the testigles.

- Some teams are best watched on teletext.

- Fat men keep off the pitch. The players may think you've got a 50/50 ball up your shirt.

- Read my lips: C H F A N C E. I know there's no 'effin chance.

- The national team manager: can't say his prayers without being quoted.

Footballers suffer from all known ailments – except a sense of shame.

Give the game back to the players: they've had everything else. (Ron Atkinson)

⚽ If your team reach the Cup Final, try to get married the same day. Then you'll never forget your wedding anniversary.

⚽ If you offer to marry any woman who can get you a cup final ticket, make sure you get a photograph – of the ticket.

⚽ Football analysts: put your money where your mouth is – up your a**e.

⚽ If you are breathalysed, say you have asthma. If you are asked for a blood sample, say you have haemophilia. If you are asked for a urine sample, say you are a City supporter.

Players can hardly read or write, but you should see them add up.

If a referee is fair, consistent and accurate he has no place on a football field.

Why bribe a goalkeeper to let in goals? Better to pay an alcoholic to have a drink.

The relationship between managers and chairmen is based on trust and understanding. The managers don't trust the chairmen and the chairmen don't understand the managers.

Lord Lucan is alive and well and living in your team's trophy room.

- Opposing fans have little respect. Some match days you can barely hear yourself abuse them.

- Archangel Gabriel: the first wing-back.

- There'll never be a decent soccer movie – until Disney get involved.

- 'You're not singing any more...' Frankly, it was risky to start.

- Forget running off the ball. You'll be lucky if they run off their lunch.

- The only difference between a hedgehog and the opposition fans' coach is that the hedgehog's pricks are on the outside.

If cash at the club gets tight, convince the board to work as film extras – in any sequel to *Jurassic Park*.

Agents: managers prefer not to use wide men in the modern game.

⚽ The footballer's wife: last year's model.

⚽ The fan's dog barks in delight when his team wins. It also turns somersaults when they lose – if it's kicked hard enough.

Cup tickets always go to the most loyal fans – of other sports.

When the cup comes home, the flags'll be flying. As will the pigs.

Things are worse when:

- Oxo plans to introduce a new cube in your team's colours. It'll be called 'laughing stock'.
- The Pools Panel award the opposition a 'walkover'.
- The manager runs on to kiss the scorer.

- John Stalker is called in to investigate your 'shoot to miss' policy.
- You get reduced admission if you bring your boots.
- You arrive and the pitch is still being ploughed.
- The ref penalises your side for 'not trying'.

- There's nothing more exhilarating than being at Wembley as your team lift the cup – until you wake up.

- Cross a chimpanzee with a goalkeeper to get a fantastically agile creature which lives in a mock-Tudor house in Hertfordshire.

Some players are like bungee jumpers – always bouncing back from suspension.

If asked what you thought of the game, say you prefer football.

Strikers and fans suffer one thing in common – a complete lack of service.

⚽ Continental refs are like rowing boats: no good without a bung.

⚽ All-seater grounds: well why should you stand for football like this?

⚽ Footballers are not the best judges of the game. You certainly won't get any long sentences.

⚽ Every team needs a mid-field genius. Getting him to put his pie down and come out of the stand is another matter.

⚽ Football stands are no place for foul and abusive language. Leave that to the players.

- If there is a fire at your ground, don't worry about the cups. Crockery is cheap and easily replaceable.

- Veteran players may be entitled to a free transfer. Ask the Council for a bus pass.

Don't mock the player with the rabbit's foot. It can't be less effective than his own.

If you want to see the team's famous hard man, don't be late.

If your team is rooted to the spot, it may be posing for a 'Spot the Ball' competition.

- Don't ask the club's kit manufacturer to change the light bulbs unless you want new ones every three months, in different colours, at £40 a time.

- Ladies: do not present your private parts for autograph. Only the rivals sign fannies.

⚽ A pre-match sex ban is justified: wives won't suffer the second-rate performances and may turn violent.

⚽ The honeymoon should always be a surprise – unless your fiancée already knows your team's in Europe.

The crowd's ability to give advice is matched only by the players' ability to ignore it.

When your useful working life is over, consider joining the club's board.

In soccer, money doesn't talk any more – it goes without saying.

Your team hits mid-table only to fall prey to a disturbing new epidemic – altitude sickness.

Some fans dream of visiting the smallest grounds in the country. Some teams make their dreams come true.

A drowning manager clutches at draws.

- The long ball game is like pouring beer down the toilet: it cuts out the middle man.

- A goalkeeper may be a little stiff from reading. Wherever he's from, give him a break.

- There's a place for the press in football but they haven't dug it yet. (Tommy Docherty)

- It's a shame when your team starts a game like Juventus and ends it like Fray Bentos. (Barry Fry)

- The FA Cup is dynamite: the great leveller.

- At a crucial moment of any game, your partner will always ask you to explain the rules.

- The veteran striker: he could have finished spectacularly but now he's passed it.

- Don't take a child to football until it knows the meaning of the word w***er. It'll only ask when it gets home.

- Sometimes teams can be too clever: they string together more passes than Greavsie on *Mastermind*.

⚽ The only good losers in football are the ones who backed the other team.

⚽ The new away strip: and you wondered what the PG Tips chimps were doing now.

⚽ Bond schemes: a licence to kill the club.

- The failed footballer: could have had any club he pleased but didn't please any.

- Some players are in a league of their own. It's the only way they can get a game.

- Players: if you save yourself for the big occasion, there'll never be one.

Aggravate the rival fan in your family: hide outside the window with the remote control.

Sometimes every match is a charity match: you're doing them a favour by showing up.

Dodgy keepers: forget the idea of throwing yourself under a bus. It will go under you.

With so many police around, how come your team is always losing its way?

'Forever blowing bubbles…': the closest some teams get is a fart in the bath after the match.

Avoid getting married on a Saturday – you may be late for the match.

- The local derby: more shameless hacks on the field than in the press box.

- The local derby: the referee is required to name his next of kin.

- The local derby: like nuclear war – no winners, only survivors.

If you want to be able to read a player's autograph, let him copy his name out of the programme.

Testimonials these days should really be called Alimonials.

Referees are wrong, even when they're right.

- The best players are either clever enough to know they can win or stupid enough not to know they can't.

- Time with the family costs you nothing: take them along to reserve fixtures.

- Roy of the Rovers would not have asked *Hello!* magazine to depict him in his 'charming Melchester home'.

- A typical defence is composed of full-backs, half-backs and drawbacks.

⚽ If you find yourself in a croc-infested swamp, keep shouting 'United for the Cup'. Not even a croc can swallow that.

⚽ If you're in intense pain, ask someone to blow three blasts on a whistle. It stops the agony every Saturday, so why not now?

Take an instant dislike to the opposition: it saves time.

Don't barrack an opposing manager. If he's fired, there's only one club that will have him...

⚽ However often your manager shuffles the pack, he always ends up with 11 jokers on the park.

⚽ It's terrible to see a player kicked where it hurts most: in the pocket.

Football: the only game where one amateur bosses 22 professionals.

Pray for a manager who doesn't think tactics are a new kind of peppermint.

⚽ Watching a game sober is like an operation without an anaesthetic.

⚽ Tippling players: if you want immortality, it's best not to try to embalm yourself first.

Things are even worse when:

- Your team gets done for tax evasion: they've been claiming for silver polish.
- Your team tries to swap shirts with the other team before the game.
- Your club is taken over – by Madame Tussaud's.

- Mulder & Scully come to investigate how you avoided relegation.
- Even the subs sneak out before full-time.
- The goalkeeper only gets a place because it is his ball.
- Some season ticket holders were caught tunnelling out of the ground.
- The manager experiments by giving the players 'flick to kick' bases.

It's no good looking for help from horoscopes. You know you can never rely on the stars.

If God had meant us to be full-backs, he'd have given us hooves.

If you want to experience life in space, go to the rival ground: there's no atmosphere.

Well-endowed women: to save embarrassment, purchase a pair of blue tits to be produced at the fans' request.

A manager loves players to express their individuality – as long as they do exactly what he says.

- Players: there will always be one person who loves you – until your mum gets a grasp of the game.

- It's a great day when you finally walk up Wembley Way, however hard it is to push your burger trolley through the fans.

- Negative equity: when fans will pay more than the asking price to see the player go.

- Players: don't object if you get pulled off at half-time. It sure beats half an orange.

A look back at the glory days of your club is a 'must' for all connoisseurs of the silent movies.

Football ground tea, coffee or Bovril are just like your team. Different cup, same s**t.

- They call your manager 'the human cannonball': he's been fired so many times.

- Some women enjoy looking at the players' legs. On a good day they may even see them move.

- When your team is losing regularly, vote with your feet: try to attend away games too.

⚽ Crop circles: the result of your team having a practice match under cover of darkness.

⚽ Players: the more you drink, the less likely you are to play the right ball. That's the one on the right.

⚽ As a last resort, a manager has his eye on a place in Europe – preferably an island.

⚽ The new 'Magic Eye' away strip: if you stare at it long enough the words 'You've been ripped off' appear.

⚽ Jesus failed to feed the 5,000 fans. The disciples had already had the five pints and two pies.

⚽ The only funeral for which you should miss a game is your own.

⚽ Football genius is one per cent inspiration and 99 per cent remuneration.

⚽ If God had meant us to eat meat, he wouldn't have given us football ground burgers.

⚽ The gentleman player: kicks your b***s off and then helps you find them after the game. (Nat Lofthouse)

⚽ Sharks will not attack a football agent: call it professional courtesy.

⚽ Why is it only when you're losing that you 'play for pride'?

- Managers leave the way they arrive
  – fired with enthusiasm. (Joe Lovejoy)

- It's time to get a new left back when milk
  turns faster.

- Players: play as if it is your last game. Or at
  least play well enough to make sure it isn't.

- Pity players with a gambling addiction. The boss told them to lose a pound or two.

- The hard man thinks that a gold card is what he gets for 100 yellows.

- Some players are as thick as a plank but none are as thick as the board.

- Dr 'Bones' McCoy on your team: 'It's football Jim, but not as we know it.'

- Sensible footballers are like squirrels: they cover their nuts.

- Pity the assistant referee: his job is on the line and the fans will not let him flag.

- Male fans: if your wife starts to show the strain, you may have to limit your children's team to six.